Table of Contents

Prologue 2
Disclaimer 3
Dedications 4
Note from the Author 5
Chapter 1 – Introduction 6
Chapter 2 - Always have a backup plan 7
Chapter 3 - Factor the unknown 11
Chapter 4 - Going fast versus getting ahead 15
Chapter 5 - Caution at the Junction 18
Chapter 6 - Accept sudden changes 21
Chapter 7 - Organize your parking 25
Chapter 8 - Learn from the past 29
Chapter 9 - Different negotiations 32
Chapter 10 - The language of the horn 35
Chapter 11 - Control the power 39
Chapter 12 - Conclusion 42
About the Author 43
Appendix 46

Prologue

Learning comes in any form in any place. A simple routine journey from home to office and back presents a host of opportunities, lessons and learnings when looked at from and in the right perspective. This journey also involves split-second decision-making that can make a huge difference.

The learnings and concepts outlined are inspired by the author's openness to travel and commute using his vehicle. He has a keen sense of direction and "traffic sense" that helps him to navigate through difficult traffic conditions without causing accidents or discomfort to anyone else.

A keen biker, he believes that going slow and steady is the core ingredient of going safe. He doesn't mind reaching his intended destination late by a few minutes instead of rushing and landing in trouble! He very strongly believes that accidents are avoidable, hence its always better and easier to be safe than sorry.

The concepts outlined are inspired from real situations from daily commute. These scenarios presented different options and the optimal option was selected based on collective judgment and decision. These were applied to various aspects of project management, which found that the projects were managed better. Some of the answers to a few questions raised during project development and execution were answered from these.

Disclaimer

Copyright © 2019 by Ayaz Zanzeria. All rights reserved worldwide. This is not a free publication. No part of this publication may be replicated, redistributed, or given away in any form without the prior written consent of the author/publisher or the terms relayed to you herein. This publication is designed to provide accurate and authoritative information about the subject matter covered. The contents of this book are based on the author's experience, original ideas and concepts. None of these have been copied from any other source. If there is a match between any part of this book and the other source, it could be either the author has given consent for his work to be published or it is a coincidence, or it has been copied without the author's knowledge.

This publication is sold in the understanding that the publisher is not engaged in rendering legal, accounting, or other professional services. If legal advice or other expert assistance is required, the services of a legal or professional should be sought. Thanks!

Dedications

This book is dedicated to my loving mother and my beloved wife who have always stood by me, through thick and thin, through adversity and prosperity, happiness and sadness, through quarrels and re-unions, etc.

Credits to my schoolteachers and school mates who have grown with me with teaching, learning, funning, punning, fighting, uniting, playing, competing, etc.

Credits to all the people around me who have stood by me through thick and thin, physically or mentally, personally or virtually, on or off social media, tenured or youngsters, etc.

Last but not the least, credits to the reader and writer, hunter and hunted, agents and supervisors, team leaders and managers, colleagues, peers and teammates, friends and acquaintances, online and offline, etc., to provide such inspiring stories and incidents for me to pen them into a book. You may or may not have served me directly or indirectly, but now it's payback time from you to me via me authoring and monetizing this book. 😊

Note from the Author

Dear Reader,

My solemn gratitude to you for taking the time to read this book. The very fact that you have opted to read this book is primarily out of curiosity or you wanted to explore and understand what you can get to learn from daily commute.

This is a form of unconventional and experiential learning. I always look around for unconventional learnings and how I can relate them with other similar events in my personal and professional life. I have found the concepts very useful and practical.

This approach has helped me effectively answer a few questions for which I would normally struggle with. A simple journey from home to office (as a routine), although overlooked by many, can be a great teacher in many aspects. This has helped me to answer a few questions about effective project management which I had successfully utilized.

Hope you do enjoy reading this book and I am sure that you will the concepts useful and relatable. Many thanks to you once again for taking the time and expressing your interest in reading this book. I am sure that you will find value in this.

Yours truly,

Ayaz Shabbir Zanzeria

Chapter 1 – Introduction

Project management is an important aspect of today's corporate, professional and business life. It is imperative that projects are planned well and executed better considering exigencies and contingencies. Although there are several institutes that teach various methods of effective project management with certifications, their effectiveness of execution varies.

In this book, an attempt has been made to relate the various aspects of project management with daily commute. A simple trip from home to office deals with different types of real situations – each of which are dealt with differently. The key is to observe closely, learn and apply the lessons learnt from these. Sometimes, they may give an answer to a difficult question. They can also hold the key to an effective alternative approach to a stalled project.

In this book, the various aspects of project management have been broken down into different key aspects in relation to the different traffic conditions. Each scenario has a few available options listed to determine the best course of action to be taken. There is no right or wrong approach, rather, the direction of the project and the outcome will determine how the overall project was managed.

The concepts presented are based on the author's personal practical experience in project management. Read on to know more about the various aspects of effective project management with the help of the lessons from commute in the subsequent chapters. These lessons and learnings are based on one continuous trip. There are many more, however, only a few key points are covered.

Chapter 2 - Always have a backup plan

Introduction

You are on the way to work. Your regular route is blocked. You must take a diversion. What do you do?

- Fight with the people who have caused the blockage.
- Take the alternate route and quickly start working on how you can reach office at the earliest, if not on time?

This forms the basis of the concept outlined in this chapter – "never be dependent on one route or person or thing". Ensure that you have an alternate route figured out and planned.

Look at available options

It's good to identify and use a route for regular commute to office and back to home. However, it is better to recognize alternate routes in case the regular route is blocked, congested or untraversable. This will ensure that you reach office no matter what. You may get late when you take an alternate route, however, your attendance in office is important instead of a lame excuse.

This applies not only to the route, albeit also the vehicle or mode of transport used. For your own vehicle, ensure that appropriate rescue options are available in case of breakdowns. For using public transport, ensure that you familiarize yourself with the various modes with their timings, availability and frequency.

Ensure that there is more than one route available from your home to your workplace. Make a careful note of the route distance, traffic conditions, congestion and other factors. This will help in better planning for contingencies. As a practice, never stick to one route only – rather, make it a habit to use different routes alternately and regularly. This will help you familiarize yourself with the different route options and the varying conditions on each.

Effectively plan for contingencies

Apply this concept to your professional life. For any company or business, "work must go on no matter what". This is a golden rule that all businesses live by. There is no people dependency, rather, there are backup and contingency plans in place. These are given different names like "business continuity plan" or "disaster management" or "disaster recovery plan" or "business contingency plan", etc. These simply focus on answering one simple question – "how does business continue in an emergency?"

Contingencies need to be planned and presented with the appropriate risks and mitigation plans for business continuity. This will help understand the impact to the business and how an additional investment can help save huge amounts of money by mitigating losses. This needs to be part of the regular process and business contingency planning.

Contingency planning in projects

Any project plan that is made, it must factor in contingencies as part of the process for effective and timely deliverance and continuity. This will automatically rule out any singular dependencies or bottlenecks that can interfere in smooth project flow. The process flow prepared will have at least two parallel paths – one main path and one contingency path. Both paths need to have some flow to avoid stagnation. There could be multiple paths depending on the business process, its scale and/or other factors.

Although the contingency path needs to be factored in the project plan, there will be similar conditions along each path. Thus, there will be one set of people working on one path and another set of people on the other path. This is to ensure that both processes are working perfectly fine. For testing, one team can stop work to check the impact on the other and vice versa. Thus, processes can be planned for smooth flow of operations with appropriate exigencies in place.

Personal life

Its always good to rule out dependencies in personal life. There is a fine line between trusting and being dependent. When someone is entrusted with a task, he/she should be made aware that they are only being trusted and not dependent upon to complete the task. Too much dependency on one person or thing leads to imminent failures and disruptions. In some cases, these can have devastating effects. Hence, it is imperative to have options open and keep a backup plan handy.

Synopsis

To conclude, always have at least two options as fallbacks for each other. Good to have multiple options, however, too many options can cause chaos. Options helps in smooth flow of operations, especially in emergencies and exigencies.

Chapter 3 - Factor the unknown

Introduction

You are on the way to work. You get caught in a traffic jam. You have no option but to wait it out. What do you do?

- Get down from the vehicle (if it's not your own) and start walking towards another mode of transport.
- Wait patiently for the traffic to subside and start moving (especially if it's your own vehicle).
- Inform your peers and stakeholders in office about the situation and your estimated time of arrival.
- Throw tantrums and vent your frustration on the people around.

In the first chapter, we saw that it is good to have a backup plan in the form of alternate routes and commute options available with proper awareness of varying conditions. In other words, rule out or minimize dependencies by having proper mitigation plans in place. This concept and approach work very well in jobs and businesses. This can help minimize delays in execution and service delivery.

Anticipate delays in planning

Whenever you plan your trip to office, calculate and factor in the additional time for unforeseen delays – such as accidents, sudden diversions and detours, etc. e.g., if your regular trip takes thirty minutes, count an additional fifteen to thirty minutes. Take additional precautionary measures as listed below.

- Leave home accordingly especially if you are using public transport or your own vehicle. If you avail company transport, you need not worry about the timing.

- Inform your peers and stakeholders about your whereabouts with an estimated time of arrival (ETA). Keep them updated on the progress of your trip and anticipated delays.
- Advise on the route taken (not mandatory, however, it is a good to do practice. This will keep your peers in the know if they must trace you in an emergency).

By following these simple but basic steps effectively, it will help you better organize and plan your trip and work.

Apply these concepts to project management

Work consists of tasks which can be grouped together to form a project. Effective project planning, development and execution means managing the sequence of tasks and their proper execution. While preparing the project charter, factor in the unforeseen delays (the 'X' factor). Prepare an execution plan accordingly with appropriate timelines. The unforeseen delays will make an allowance for the additional buffer time.

Once project development and execution begin, keep the concerned stakeholders informed and updated regularly on the progress. Prepare an ongoing or rolling project status report to be circulated at the end of every week to all the concerned stakeholders and people involved in the project. This will help effectively monitor the progress of the project and will report any delays with appropriate mitigation plans and action items.

A good project report should have the below elements:

1. Project information
    a. Project title
    b. Project lead
    c. Project sponsor
    d. Project budget and cost
    e. Status report date
2. Status summary
    a. Major accomplishments

      b. Risks and opportunities
      c. Execution plan for coming week
3. Milestones and progress
      a. List of tasks
      b. Assigned to
      c. Due date (when the task is expected to complete)
      d. Forecast date (when this task was forecast to complete)
      e. Comments to mention reasons for delay, if any.

This project report is very effective in tracking and monitoring the progress of any project in a simplistic manner. Risks can be effectively minimized with proper course corrections and mitigation plans as they are continuously identified and reported during various stages of project development and execution.

In personal life, it is imperative to keep the concerned people updated on the progress on the task. It could be for buying a house, or getting interior decoration work done, or investing money for savings. In either scenario, always good to keep family members updated on the progress.

Synopsis

It's a good practice to implement the below points for effective commute and project development and execution.

- Factor in the unforeseen.
- Allow the project to take its controlled course.
- Keep the stakeholders regularly updated on the progress.

These are simple points that indicate the basics and ground rules to be followed. It's good to be optimistic, however, it's better to also plan for the unknown. This will avoid unpleasant surprises.

Running Late On Daily Commute

Though the commute is daily and very well known, each day comes with a surprise.

You may run late on some random day.

✅ Notify your destination in-charge earlier.

✅ It will hardly take few seconds or utmost a minute to notify your destination in-charge that you are running late. Your Integrity.

This small gesture shows your
Integrity
and increases your
Dignity

Lessons from Commute

Chapter 4 - Going fast versus getting ahead

Introduction

You are at a traffic signal. It turns green. What do you do?

- ➢ Press the accelerator and zoom past the other vehicles, honking impatiently at whoever crosses your way.
- ➢ Get ready to move forward slowly or moderately with caution without endangering the lives of other pedestrians or motorists.

You are driving along. There is another vehicle in front. You want to overtake but are not able to. What do you do?

- ➢ Vent your frustration on the horn and remain behind him.
- ➢ Try to overtake dangerously either from the left or the right.
- ➢ Assess the traffic and road conditions and tag along behind.
- ➢ Overtake at the opportune moment – either at a speed breaker or at an intersection.

This is a commonly faced situation by vehicle owners in traffic. There is a tendency to race past or simply blow the horn incessantly. The real question to be asked is, is it worth the effort if it gets you into trouble?

Going fast or getting ahead?

While driving, the question to be answered is, "are you driving to go fast or to get ahead?" There is a huge difference between the two. Consider the second scenario outlined in the introduction of this chapter. The intent is to overtake the person in front who is driving at a comparatively lower speed than you. The key is to not go fast but to pause, fall back, regroup and then try again to overtake at the right time and place.

Driving requires skill and tact. It's not about unleashing the potential of your vehicle simply because it is powerful. Rather, use your intellect to control the vehicle and get ahead as per the road and prevalent driving conditions. Apply your driving skills, tact and intellectual judgment to navigate effectively to get ahead of the other vehicles and motorists.

Application in project management

Project management also involves skills, tact and intellectual judgment to navigate and execute effectively. Project progress has its own pace which needs to be regulated appropriately. This is very much like driving in traffic. The project manager is akin to the person behind the wheel.

There will be a phase during project development and execution in which the pace will become slow, causing delays. This should have been factored in during the planning phase. However, it is at this time, that the pace should not be forced as it may be due to uncontrollable factors (the 'X' factor). The key is to identify the bottlenecks and rectify them to normalcy. This is where continuous monitoring and effective project management play a crucial role.

Getting ahead is a strategy that involves pausing, assessing and restarting. This is essential as it involves continuous monitoring and appropriate course correction where necessary to maintain the project on track. The approach of moving forward with a strategy in place will help you to get ahead without going very fast.

Synopsis

Going fast is simply going quickly or rapidly at a high risk, whereas getting ahead is strategy based in which you look for the right moment to move ahead of competition. It's easy to go fast and land in trouble. However, when proper strategies are applied and executed to get ahead, they are more effective as they will help you move in a more controlled and organized manner.

Going Fast Vs Going Ahead

There is a huge difference in both

Going fast leads you to cut the distance

 Going ahead makes you to effectively walk the path

Going fast is all about time

 Going ahead is all about strategy and efficiency

Chapter 5 - Caution at the Junction

Introduction

You are driving along the road. You are approaching a junction. There are people and/or vehicles crossing. What do you do?

- Start blowing the horn ferociously to announce your arrival.
- Speed up to make the pedestrians move fast out of fear to clear the way for you to pass.
- Slow down to a stop, let the junction clear and then pass.

This is a beautiful example of a situation in which an accident can be easily avoided by exercising a little bit of caution and common sense.

Approach with caution

Whenever you approach any junction, proceed with caution. You never know when an obstacle will suddenly confront you. Hence, whenever you approach a junction, reduce your speed and brace yourself for any sudden stops or jerks. Blow your horn in intermittent intervals, look in all directions and ascertain that it is safe to proceed. Caution to be taken to also look for other vehicles from different directions. Then proceed forward as per normal driving and traffic conditions.

This is a simple and best approach to cross a junction. A little delay can go a long way in ensuring a safe and smooth ride without endangering the lives of pedestrians and/or other motorists. Another factor to consider is that some of the pedestrians may be handicapped or too fragile to move fast. There could also be someone on a wheelchair, or a lady with her infant kid, or someone who has difficulty in walking quick. Hence, it is better to slow down and allow them to pass to avoid endangering innocent lives. They too have a right of way on the road. As a humane gesture, you may even get down from your vehicle and offer help to someone crossing.

Application to project development and execution

During the project development and execution phase, it is always imperative to have the project plan and charter with you. This will ensure that you are aware of the project "route" or "path". During the execution and development, there will be junctions on the way. Approach these with caution. Assess and ascertain the junction for stoppages and impacts. Work out the mitigation to minimize or negate the assessed risks.

This is a crucial step for the smooth flow of the project development and execution. A good project manager always needs to be on top of the project execution path or course by continuously gathering and monitoring data. The stakeholders involved need to be kept in the loop by means of regular communication and status reports. Team members pace of working also needs to be factored in to determine the pace of progress.

In personal life, there will be times when such junctions must be crossed. A classic example is what do you do with a sum of money, especially with a milestone coming up (marriage, college admission, migration to another place, etc.). This is where you assess the merits and demerits of each option at this junction and take a decision accordingly as per merit.

Synopsis

Approach a junction with caution. Blow the horn to announce your arrival, however, do not cause a nuisance. Respect the other's right to use the road also. Similarly, during the project progress, be mindful of the junctions and the hindrances that it may offer. Respect them and mitigate them as per merit. Empower your team members to take small independent decisions. Keep the stakeholders in the loop with regular communication and detailed status reports. Form communication and focus groups to make this more effective.

Chapter 6 - Accept sudden changes

Introduction

You are approaching the traffic signal. Your regular route is to take a right. However, the traffic policeman is diverting all vehicles to the left as the route towards the right has been restricted. What do you do?

- Argue with the traffic policeman for diverting the traffic.
- Try and force your way through to the right.
- Go with the flow and take the left. Do a course correction and look for a better and faster route to get to office at the earliest.

Sudden changes to regular routine tend to cause disruption, however, they also trigger immediate adjustments. They instigate you to think at the tip of your toes for a quick fix to an immediate problem. The adaptability towards change will determine your approach towards challenges.

Sudden changes are unforeseen

When you travel by one route daily, you feel that you know the route and conditions like the back of your hand. However, it comes as a rude shock when you suddenly must take a detour. Simply because you did not see it coming or you were ignorant towards it. In either case, the situation is present which needs to be dealt with. Refer to chapter two of this book in which we had stressed on the importance of an alternate route.

Sudden changes or the 'X' factor tend to play an important role in determining the course of the project. They can cause course corrections or disruptions depending on the magnitude and impact. The key is to identify these based on experience, data and analytics. Once they have been identified, they must be planned and factored. These can be accommodated either at the very outset or during the project progress at any stage.

Importance and use of risk register

Unknown factors can be assessed in the form of risks. Risk identification and mitigation is a critical aspect of project planning. When preparing the project charter, make a risk register. This will outline the below points. Enlisting the risks with their impacts will help to devise a mitigation plan, which can be factored in the primary project plan.

1) Name and nature of the risk
2) Risk assessment
    a. Probability of occurrence
    b. Impact of occurrence
3) Damage/losses caused
4) Risk mitigation and management
    a. Risk owner
    b. Mitigation due date
    c. Impact quantification or explanation
    d. Action items for mitigation
    e. Known monetary valuation
    f. Unknown monetary valuation

The primary importance of the risk register to curb losses and/or damages while ensuring business continuity. Risk management is an important aspect of the business, especially when managed well. One of the destructive powers of uncontrolled risk is that it erodes profit, profitability and trust. Hence, when projects are planned, risks also need to be identified and planned.

This can be colour coded to determine the impact of each risk and how it can be mitigated. Proper maintenance of this risk register can help to embrace the impact of sudden changes. The risk needs to be expressed in simple terms to effectively mitigate it. The risk register attempts to highlight the impact of the risk and to maintain a simple mitigation plan. Some risks would require an ongoing process to minimize the impact and some would require intermittent activities, and some would need a one-time setup. Hence, each risk can be mitigated, minimized and managed.

Stakeholders or team members are identified to mitigate and manage the various risks involved. They would be accountable for ensuring that their respective risks are managed well. Each mitigation action item has timelines attached to it which makes for better planning. Some of these action items can be discrete, some are ongoing, some need to be executed at regular intervals.

Synopsis

To summarize, each sudden change can be prepared for with proper project planning with project charter and risk register as two essential elements of the project plan. Risks need to be identified and mitigated to minimize business losses and/or damages. This will help to accept and embrace the changes encountered at any time.

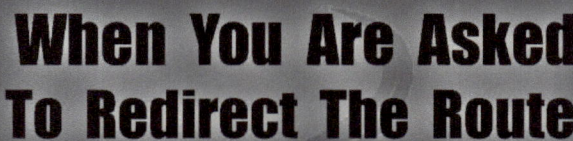

Chapter 7 - Organize your parking

Introduction

You have reached your destination. You are in the parking lot searching for a place to park. You find an open parking spot. What do you do?

- ➤ You park your vehicle in a hurry without worrying about how you have parked. The way you have parked your vehicle occupies more space than usual and can cause inconvenience to other motorists.
- ➤ You take some time to park your vehicle properly so as not to cause inconvenience to others.
- ➤ Look for an attendant to help park your vehicle.

The way you park your vehicle in the available parking space speaks about how organized or chaotic your thought process is. It also indicates whether you are self-centered or considerate.

Optimize available space

When there is an open space available with minimal usage, there is a tendency to occupy the maximum available space. This means that the vehicle "hogs" the parking space thereby disallowing other vehicles to be parked near it. This appears to be "inconsiderate behavior" of the vehicle owner. Invariably, vehicle owners tend to park with minimal time and rush away. When they are approached by the parking attendant, they always ignore or shoo them away on the pretext of "a couple of minutes" or "five minutes". However, they always take more time than that.

On the other hand, when there is limited parking available, vehicle owners tend to be more careful in maneuvering the vehicle in the appropriate parking space. This is when the true driving skills surface as the navigation between closely parked vehicles relies more on judgment and tact. The same precaution and approach need to be taken when there is plenty of open parking space available. Its good to be organized even when parking your vehicle.

Organizing your project

Apply the same concept to project management. Any project will have several files that need to be created. These are in the form of excel spreadsheets, powerpoint presentations, word documents, etc. all these need to be properly labeled and organized in separate folders. Any information about any project at any stage of progress should be readily available at your fingertips.

A properly documented project should have the below documents. This is an indicative list and is neither exhaustive nor exclusive. There could be other documents not listed here.

- Project requisition form.
- Project proposal.
- SOW (Statement of Work).
- Specification documents.
    - Design requirements.
    - Functional specifications.
    - Program structure.
    - Database structure and administration.
    - Reporting and analytics.
- Project charter with milestones and timelines.
- Risk register.
- Gantt chart.
- Status reports.
- Change requisitions.
- SOP (Standard Operating Procedure).
- Training documents (word documents and/or presentations).
- Any other supporting documents.
- Data and analytics working files.
- Testing, evaluations and results files.

Each project should have a corresponding folder structure to organize and secure the related files in them. Some of these documents are standard in terms of the information and layout while some are created on the fly based on requirements of the project. Data files should be appropriately named and organized. Additional caution must be exercised when dealing with data as it can be sensitive. Effective organization of these documents will help in efficient management and control of the project development and execution along its course and beyond.

Synopsis

Always be organized in various aspects of project management – especially in the documentation. All the necessary and related documents need to be properly organized and stored securely in an appropriate folder structure. Appropriate accesses with varying permissions need to be given to the respective stakeholders.

Chapter 8 - Learn from the past

Introduction

You are driving along your lane in the road. There is a vehicle closing behind you wanting to overtake you. What do you do?

- Continue driving in your lane. Ignore his honking.
- Look in the rear-view mirror and see which side he is approaching from. Drive towards the other lane to make way for him to pass.
- Look in the rear-view mirror to watch him and avert his chances of overtaking you. Do not let him pass.

Good to move forward with an eye on the rear. This does the below:

- Keeps you wary of what is happening behind you.
- Learn from past mistakes and apply them moving forward.
- The pace and direction of forward movement sometimes depends on the vision the rear-view mirror projects.

Rear view mirror is a metaphor which means to look back in the past and learn from the journey. In other words, assess the progress, applaud the good and work on the areas of improvements.

In the literal sense, when you look in the rear-view mirror of a vehicle while driving, you are simply being wary of the vehicles behind you. This helps you to drive forward with caution and take evasive action where necessary. This is essential for safe driving and can help avoid accidents.

Project management

As the project development and execution progresses, it is imperative to review the progress periodically. Ideally, progress review should happen every week with a fair assessment of what went right and what could have been done better.

Enlist the things that happened right – this forms the basis of doing them better by doing them differently. Enlist the areas of improvements – this will give a list of things to be avoided and done differently. In either scenario, the way the tasks were executed need to be scanned for areas of opportunity, irrespective of how they were done in the previous review cycle. This forms the basis of continuous improvement.

This is the concept of the rear-view mirror as a metaphor. It symbolizes to look back and reflect. Regular appraisals and reviews in project progress indicate continuous internal and external monitoring to continuously do better. Apply this to all aspects of the project development and execution cycle. Out of five days of the week, four days should be for the actual development and execution, the fifth day should be for review and status update. There can be two types of review – internal review within the core project team and an external review with the external stakeholders.

Continuous review cycle also helps control the project participants. It ensures that everyone know their tasks and roles. How they execute it depends on their individual intellect, skill and tact. The project manager must determine the abilities and limitations of his team and how he can nurture their skills and talents. Thus, the rear-view mirror concept helps to look back to progress forward with caution and care.

Synopsis

Hence, we have stressed on the importance of the rear-view mirror aspect of project management. This gives the opportunity to review in a bid to do things differently and do them better. Continuous monitoring, review and improvement in a project, builds the stakeholders confidence in the team to handle the project effectively and efficiently.

Chapter 9 - Different negotiations

Introduction

You are driving towards the office. You approach a curve with three lanes. What do you do?

- Take the innermost lane as it is the shortest.
- Take the outermost as it can allow you to drive fast.
- Take the middle as it has the least traffic.

Different road conditions require you to take different lanes at varying speeds. Another factor to consider is to focus on and stick to one lane while traversing the curve. This would require constant regulation of speed – slowing down or speeding up appropriately.

Driving in traffic always poses varying conditions on any type of road – straight or curved, narrow or wide, smooth or potholed, etc. It is imperative that we are always attentive to the varying conditions and drive accordingly. Negotiating curves and bends requires extra caution and attention. The primary need is to maintain the vehicle in one lane at the appropriate speed.

Negotiating as per merit

Apply this principle to project management. The same concept must be negotiated with different people in different ways. There is no "one size fits all" approach. Thus, if a set of tasks need to be executed differently, the stakeholders must be negotiated with in one way. The peers and project team members must be negotiated with another manner. Both are different individuals, hence two different approaches. The way each road is treated, each person or stakeholder or project participant must be treated differently as per merit.

This leads to meticulous preparation of various types of reports based on different types of analytics, visualizations and storytelling. Reports, presentations and storyboards are key tools and documents that help to effectively narrate and negotiate. Different stakeholders require different type of presentations and reports. This is where the knowledge of different types of tools makes a difference. These help in formulating different approaches and methods of analysis for the same data set. Once the analysis has been done, list down the observations and inferences, and devise an action plan.

Tools and documents for negotiation

Once this presentation is prepared with the weekly status report or as part of it, this can be effectively used to negotiate with the internal project team and external stakeholders. The way the presentation and the message are conveyed will vary in both scenarios for both. This is where negotiation skills play a vital role. Effective project management involves appropriate negotiation.

Why negotiation? There will be resistance of different types from both ends – from the stakeholders and the team members. If the ideas and concepts are feasible and viable, they need to be communicated and negotiated for approval from both. The stakeholders for budgeting and the project team for execution.

Synopsis

Treat each road and traffic condition as per merit. Similarly, when dealing with different members of a project team, each person needs to be given due credit and respect when dealing with them. At every level, every person is different, hence everyone must be treated as per merit, rank, credibility, designation, knowledge, skillset, etc.

NEGOTIATING TURNS

When we reach a curve,
whether you take the inner path
or outer path,
depends on situation.

YOUR DECISION DECIDES YOUR PATH

Indeed, may it be
a road or life,
your decisions
of few moments
decide everything
about the
further path.

Chapter 10 - The language of the horn

Introduction

You are caught in a traffic jam. Vehicles are moving slowly. There is bumper to bumper traffic. What do you do?

- Be patient and move forward slowly with the flow.
- Blow your horn ferociously.
- Honk only when needed.
- Vent your frustration on the steering wheel.

Invariably, on any road where there are vehicles, especially traffic, the sounds of the horn tend to drown other sounds. The horn has developed its own language. This language depicts the different moods, emotions and frames of minds of the various motorists involved.

Language of the horn

Depending on person and mindset, traffic conditions and other factors, there are different "moods" that are depicted by the horn as listed below.

- Short beep
- 2 short successive beeps
- A 5-10-second-long beep
- A 5-10 second continuous beep followed by short bursts of beeps
- A long 20-30 second continuous beep
- Series of 5-10 second beeps

These are some of the commonly heard horn sounds with their durations and frequencies. Each of these depict different moods and mindsets of the drivers and honkers. This is a language that has silently evolved and developed. People across the globe know this universal language without learning it as its comprehension and interpretation is simple.

Emotional Intelligence

One way of looking at the language of the horn is that it displays lack of emotional intelligence to a certain extent. Emotional intelligence (EI) is defined as the capacity to be aware of and control the expression of one's emotions, to handle interpersonal relationships with empathy and justice. In a nutshell, EI consists of five components listed below as per Daniel Goleman.

- Self-awareness – be clear of what you feel and why.
- Self-regulation – accept defeat with grace and dignity.
- Motivation – to look at things and situations positively.
- Empathy – understand the other by walking in their shoes.
- Social Skills – be happy to mingle with other people by respecting their viewpoints and perspectives.

These are some of the basic concepts of EI. These can be effectively used to counter the "language of the horn" under all circumstances. There are different metrics defined to measure and gauge the levels of EI of an individual. However, that is an indicative scale. We will limit the discussion of EI in this chapter and book.

Application of Emotional Intelligence

During the project development and execution cycle, there are times when the project manager and all the different people involved, undergo different emotional transitions. The way they vent out or express themselves is very similar to the language of the horn. Hence, it is imperative for the other members to keep calm and display a high level of emotional intelligence.

There are plenty of institutes and courses that teach various forms of emotional intelligence. This is an important aspect of human behavior that helps in controlling the emotions of the different team members.

The course of the project will instigate different emotions – happiness, sadness, anger, frustration, disappointment, etc. Each of these will trigger different reactions and modes of expression by different individuals involved. It's ok to express oneself as we are all humans. However, all these need to be moderated considering work ethics. Emotional intelligence and different styles of leadership combined can help to curb and channelize the expression and display of emotions.

Synopsis

The horn has its own "silent" language, which does not need learning for understanding, interpretation or decoding. Similarly, project development and execution have an underlying "silent" language that can be understood and controlled with the help of Emotional Intelligence. An important aspect to consider is to "agree to disagree" as a form of respect. This will help avoid conflicts during the project cycle and beyond.

Horn - They are usually irritating and symbolizes panics.

Be it be due to time or other priorities.

Loud Voices - As you become clueless and helpless during traffic, same goes with life in same situations.

You tend to raise your voice due to increased anxiety.

Stay calm in traffic and stuck phases. It will pass by silently.

Chapter 11 - Control the power

Introduction

You are waiting at a traffic signal on your new powerful bike. It turns green. What do you do?

- Rev up your bike and race off ahead of the others.
- Start moving forward, however, with caution and control.

Vehicles nowadays are powerful especially in terms of their pickup and racing abilities. Although they do have several safety features, however, the power control lies in the hands of the rider.

Control the power

Any vehicle is powerful. Hence, the drivers of the vehicles must undergo a proper training to understand how the vehicle works and how it can be controlled. People can learn basic driving skills within a couple of hours in which they can learn how to start a vehicle, drive it, maneuver it and stop it. For proper navigation and driving within real traffic and driving conditions, it can take at least a month of practice. After that, it is upto the individual on how he chooses to drive the vehicle.

The rider of the vehicle has an idea about the vehicle's power and capability and unleashes it accordingly. He has the choice to either be reckless with it or be cautious. This would mean the difference between being responsible and being careless. Any vehicle comes with power. With power comes responsibility that needs to be handled with caution and care. Important to control the power and not let it control you.

Responsibilities in project management

Project management comes with a set of responsibilities as listed below. This list is indicative, it is not exclusive or exhaustive.

- Proper documentation.
- Timely reporting.
- Appropriate and timely communication.
- Active participation.
- Accountability and responsibility.
- Decision making.
- Team management.
- Client management.
- Relationship management.

All of these are part of the project management cycle and need to be fulfilled responsibly. Generally, project teams tend to divide these amongst themselves for efficient fulfilment. This is one approach. Another approach is that the project manager overseas the project flow and completes all of these by himself. There are other approaches depending on the school of thought and mutual agreement within the team.

Effectively, the project team is given a special set of responsibilities to handle that may supersede any other regular authority of their peers. Care needs to be taken to understand these and exercise these with care. These should not be abused or misused at any time. The project lead or project manager is the driver of his team and power. He needs to exercise proper controls with appropriate protocols to remain in control. He should not let the team control him else the project will go out of control. He needs to lead by example by exercising responsible use of power.

Synopsis

Control the power, don't let it control you. This should be the "mantra" of any good project management team and any other person. With power comes responsibility which must be fulfilled with care and caution. There are different tools, mechanisms and approaches available either singly or in combinations that help you to achieve this.

CONTROL THE POWER

When you have a powerful vehicle, there is a tendency to get lost in the power that you tend to forget your responsibilities.

Always be in control of the power and authority that is bestowed upon you.

The higher you go
in terms of designations,
the more authority and power you get.

Chapter 12 - Conclusion

Thus, we saw how various situations and scenarios presented to us as part of our daily commute pose options. The selection of the appropriate one depends on the individual's judgment and tact. To reiterate, there is no wrong or right selection. However, the outcome of the selection will determine the tact of the intellect displayed.

Sometimes, answers to difficult questions do not come directly, albeit indirectly. Learnings and lessons from commute tend to be highly overlooked and ignored by many. When looked at in the right perspective and frame of mind, they can answer questions that are otherwise difficult.

Along similar lines, these situations are akin to part of the project management, development and execution life cycle. Simply done well, they can go a long way in handling projects efficiently and effectively. Listed below are some of the different aspects of the project management cycle that we get to learn from a simple commute from home to office.

- Plan for backups and contingencies. Remove dependencies.
- Give an allowance for the 'X' factor – the unknown.
- Continuously assess, recoup and restart to maintain the pace.
- Pause at important junctures and milestones.
- Be ready to accept sudden course diversions during the project development and/or execution life cycle.
- Use the risk register for effective risk mitigation.
- Be organized – control the chaos.
- Reflect from the project inception till the current status to assess for areas of improvement.
- Different situations require different types of negotiations.
- Communicate differently with different people. This is part of treating everyone equally.
- Be responsible with the power and authority granted to you. Don't let the power control you. Don't abuse the power.

About the Author

Ayaz is an out of the box thinker and loves to look beyond the obvious. He has the uncanny knack of spotting things where people generally overlook or oversee. He is an avid fan of continuous learning and firmly believes that every interaction is a learning experience. Hence, he seeks to learn something new from everyone every day.

During his professional career, he has consistently delivered award-winning performances as an eminent team-player. Often, he has been an unsung hero – delivering performances without hogging the limelight. He has come across many managers with different managing styles and approaches, the good, the bad and the ugly. He has chosen to extract, learn and implement the good from each.

He believes that entrepreneurship is a thought process and a lifestyle that can be adopted by anyone and applied to personal and professional life. He had his stints of entrepreneurship from the early stages of his life. He had learnt a bit about business the old-fashioned way from his father. He had learnt how to manage a distributed setup and different people in different locations.

Amongst one of his earlier ventures was that of an internet café or a cybercafé, which did not give him the returns as he had envisaged. Nevertheless, he had not let his failure bog him down. Rather, he simply moved on to get a job and advance his career. He took all his jobs as learning various aspects of the business, the different sub-entities within the larger umbrella and how they gel together.

Armed with that knowledge and experience, he is currently heading two ventures:

1. **ZANZERIA FAMILY CONSULTANTS (OPC) Pvt Ltd.**
    a. Written and Media Content Development.
    b. Specializing in short text/musical videos.
    c. Tutorial Video Series.
    d. Visual representations – static or graphical.
    e. Personal Finance Management.
    f. Mentoring and Consulting.

    Tag Line: **a written and media content development studio**

    Associated Brand(s):

    - **Artismatic Magnifico** – artistic creativity in its charismatic magnificence.

2. **INMUTATIO CONSULERE Pvt Ltd.**
    a. Business Process Improvement.
    b. Voice of Customer Analysis.
    c. Customer Experience Enhancement Program.
    d. Business Publications.
    e. Leadership and Organizational Development.
    f. Corporate Branding and Communication.

    Tag Line: **re-imagine » re-think » re-engineer**

    Associated Brand(s):

    - **Azimuth** – Customer Driven Initiatives to Improve Business Processes
    - **Chrysalis** – Enhancing Leadership Skills for Effective Change Management
    - **Lexicon** – Redefining Corporate Communications

A bit about his history, he was born and brought up in the Island city of Mumbai where he spent nearly 35 years of his life. He has worked in several companies in different roles and fulfilled different responsibilities as required by the businesses.

The primary strength that Ayaz has is the ability to learn quickly. He has not done too many courses apart from completing his Bachelor's in Automobile Engineering. All his skills have been acquired and polished practically on the job.

Ayaz is straightforward and blunt, which is resented by many. He firmly believes that an initial ugly bluntness is far better than hidden rosy falseness. It is this approach coupled with a never give up attitude and approach that has kept him going through various hardships of life.

He has been approached by many for various reasons. For consulting, mentoring, counselling, advice, business partnerships, business projects, to name a few. He was involved in founding and setting up a few companies from which he has moved out for various reasons (personal and professional).

Although not very good at marketing or selling, he has an uncanny knack of striking good conversations even with little knowledge of the topic. He believes that learning is a never-ending process that never stops at any age or designation. Another reason for being open to learning is his belief in change is constant. Change is inevitable and will happen. Hence, rather than resist change, welcome it with open arms.

Ayaz does not believe in money making gimmicks or get rich quick schemes. Rather he prefers to take the slow and steady consistent and sustainable approach for making money. He has tried this approach with his knowledge of share trading which is paying him rich dividends.

Appendix

The simplest way is to find Ayaz is to type "Ayaz Zanzeria" in google search. The search results will give a listing of all his websites, social media profiles and other listings on other websites. Specific contact info is as below.

Company Websites

- ❖ https://thezanzeriafamily.com
- ❖ https://artismatic.gallery
- ❖ https://inmutatio.com

Personal Websites

- ❖ https://ayazzanzeria.page
- ❖ https://thejanz.rocks

Professional Contact

- ❖ ayaz@thezanzeriafamily.com
- ❖ ayaz@inmutatio.com
- ❖ Call/Text/WhatsApp: +91 80955 03465 / +91 63606 17899
- ❖ Skype: ayaz.zanzeria / ayaz@thezanzeriafamily.com

Personal Contact

- ❖ hi@ayazzanzeria.page
- ❖ ayaz@thejanz.rocks
- ❖ ayaz.zanzeria@hotmail.com
- ❖ ayazzanzeria@gmail.com

www.ingramcontent.com/pod-product-compliance
Lightning Source LLC
Chambersburg PA
CBHW040247220526
45473CB00001B/404